Who Was
Ernest Hemingway?

by Jim Gigliotti

illustrated by Gregory Copeland

Penguin Workshop

For Dante, a man of courage—JG

For my wonderful mother, for everything
(or all?) you've done for me—GC

PENGUIN WORKSHOP
An imprint of Penguin Random House LLC, New York

First published in the United States of America by Penguin Workshop,
an imprint of Penguin Random House LLC, New York, 2022

Text copyright © 2022 by Jim E. Gigliotti
Illustrations copyright © 2022 by Penguin Random House LLC

Visit us online at penguinrandomhouse.com.

Library of Congress Cataloging-in-Publication Data is available.

Printed in the United States of America

ISBN 9780399544132 (paperback)   10 9 8 7 6 5 4 3 2 1 WOR
ISBN 9780399544156 (library binding)   10 9 8 7 6 5 4 3 2 1 WOR

Contents

Who Was Ernest Hemingway? 1

Young Storyteller 7

Early Writings 19

Love and War 28

To Paris 38

World Traveler 53

New Adventures 68

War Correspondent 81

Triumph and Tragedy 93

Timelines 106

Bibliography 108

Who Was Ernest Hemingway?

The big bear stopped in the middle of the road. It was somewhere "out West," Ernest Hemingway said. It might have been in Idaho, or maybe it was Montana. The bear stood on its hind legs. It roared at any car that tried to pass by. The bear would not budge. The cars either turned back or went the long way around. After a while, no one could use the road. All the drivers were scared of the huge animal.

But not Ernest. He wasn't scared. He was mad. He drove right up to where the bear was standing. He got out of his car and yelled at the beast. What did the animal think it was doing? "Do you realize that you're nothing but a miserable, common black bear?" Ernest said.

The bear went down from its hind legs. It

slinked to the side of the road on all fours. It never bothered the cars again.

Did this story really happen?

Ernest sure could tell it like it had. That was his great gift: He was an amazing storyteller.

Ernest liked to tell his friends about the time he landed the biggest sailfish ever caught in the Atlantic Ocean. Then there was the time he

claimed to have met enemy spy Mata Hari during World War I. And the time he saved an African village from a lion that was lurking near its fields at night. Some of the stories were true. Most were a *little* bit true. A few weren't true at all.

But Ernest wasn't known all around the world because he told stories about himself to his friends. He became famous because he wrote books and  stories that are still read by millions of people today, more than sixty years after his death. He wrote *The Sun Also Rises*, *A Farewell to Arms*, *The Old Man and the Sea*—some of the best-known books in American literature. In all, he wrote more than twenty books and more than fifty short stories.

Most of Ernest's books and stories were fiction, which means they were made up. But they all seem to have in them some details of events that really happened to Ernest.

He really did travel to Spain for the bullfights, like the people in *The Sun Also Rises*. He was on the front lines of World War I, like his main character in *A Farewell to Arms*. He worked hard to catch huge fish in the ocean, like the fisherman in *The Old Man and the Sea*. Sometimes it was hard to tell where real events stopped and the fiction began.

Ernest was always in search of adventure. He looked for situations that would test his courage and his ability to perform under pressure. Then he used those experiences to write stories that are still meaningful to readers today.

However, his stories aren't important only

for *what* he wrote about. They also are important for *how* he wrote them. Ernest wrote in a new way, with short sentences that got right to the point. He didn't use many adjectives to describe things. And he often didn't choose to use big words.

Ernest Hemingway became one of the most important authors in American history. His unique style has influenced many other writers— even to this day.

CHAPTER 1
Young Storyteller

When Ernest Hemingway was a little boy, his mother once asked him what he was afraid of.

"'Fraid a nothin'!" Ernest said.

That was the truth! Young Ernest would try just about anything. He was only three years old when he went fishing for the first time. Not long after that, he learned to start a campfire. By the time he was five, he knew how to hunt.

Ernest was born on July 21, 1899, in Oak Park, Illinois, not far from the city of Chicago. His father, Clarence Edmonds Hemingway, usually called Ed, was a doctor. His mother, Grace, was a music teacher. She had dreamed of being an opera singer when she was younger. When Ernest was born, the Hemingway family lived with Grace's father. Ed and Grace had fallen in love when the doctor was a regular visitor at the house to care for Grace's mom, who was sick. Grace's mom died in 1895. Ed and Grace were married the next year.

Ed and Grace Hemingway

Ernest with his parents and siblings

Ernest had an older sister, Marcelline. He had three younger sisters: Ursula was born three years after Ernest. Madelaine was born in 1904. Carol was born in 1911. Leicester (say: Lester) was born in 1915, when Ernest was a teenager.

Marcelline was eighteen months old when Ernest was born. Grace had been hoping for another daughter. She wanted to have two little girls whom she could dress alike. And even though Ernest turned out to be a boy, that didn't stop Grace. She dressed Ernest like a girl.

That wasn't unusual for the time. Many families dressed boys just like girls when they were babies. But Grace dressed Ernest and Marcelline in matching pink outfits and called them her "two summer girls." *That* was unusual. Grace sometimes still had Earnest wear girls' clothes up until he was almost six years old.

Ernest's father didn't like that idea. Neither did Ernest. He was a rough-and-tumble boy who liked to hunt, fish, and play outdoors.

In fact, every summer Ed took Grace and the children out to the country to a family cottage at Walloon Lake in Michigan. Ernest's first trip to

Michigan came only six weeks after he was born.
He would return every summer for eighteen years.

There was no dressing up Ernest in girl clothes
at Walloon Lake. There, Ernest hunted and fished.
His father taught him how to use a gun.

One summer day when Ernest was a young

boy, he was running with a stick in his mouth. He fell down. The stick cut into the back of his throat. Luckily, Ed knew what to do.

He removed the stick and fixed the wound. Ernest's injury healed. But it was the first of many serious accidents he would have in his life.

Back in Oak Park, Ernest started first grade in 1905. He was a good student. After school, Grace made him practice playing the cello in the big new house the family had moved into earlier that year. The house was three stories high and had eight bedrooms. It had a separate music room in which Grace could give lessons. But Ernest hated playing the cello! He wanted to be outside with his friends, running around and playing sports. And if he couldn't be so active, he wanted to be reading.

Ernest read almost anything he could get his hands on. But he especially liked adventure stories. *Robinson Crusoe* was one of his favorite books. It is a story by Daniel Defoe about a man shipwrecked on an island. Another author, Robert Louis Stevenson, wrote many of the other adventure stories that Ernest liked.

Those books helped develop Ernest's great

imagination. One day when he was five years old, he raced in the door of the house. He excitedly told his family how he had stopped a runaway horse all by himself!

"This boy is going to be heard from some day," Ernest's grandfather told Grace. "If he uses his imagination for good purposes, he'll be famous."

Each year before the family went to Walloon Lake, Ernest made a trip to the library in Oak Park. He checked out as many books as he could carry. The rest of the summer, whenever he wasn't out hunting or fishing, he spent his time with a good book.

CHAPTER 2
Early Writings

Ernest entered Oak Park High School in the fall of 1913. He began writing for the school paper, the *Trapeze*. His first assignment was to report about a concert at the school. But he soon discovered that his real talent was for making up stories. Luckily, his high school also had a magazine.

His first short story was written for the school's magazine, which was called the *Tabula*. It was about a hunter who set a trap for a fellow hunter, only to be caught up in it himself, too. Ernest's short stories for the *Tabula* were often about sports or the outdoors.

Ernest was on the swim team and in the rifle club. He made up stories about the rifle club to fill space in the *Trapeze*. He also told tales about being a football star. In reality, Ernest was no star. He liked football because he was big and strong, and he could use that to his advantage. But he was not especially fast. He played on the lightweight team his sophomore and junior seasons. The lightweight team was a notch below the top level in high school, like junior varsity is to varsity now. Ernest made the top team in his final year.

By that time, Ernest already stood about five feet ten inches tall. He had lots of friends, and the girls thought he was handsome. However, he was shy around them. When it was time for a school dance, he helped decorate the school gymnasium but then left before the dance began.

In the classroom, Ernest earned high marks in English and history. His grades were good enough for him to go to college. It wasn't as common in the early part of the twentieth century as it is now for high-school seniors to go on to college.

Still, Ernest's family expected that is what he would do after graduation. His father hoped that Ernest would go on to become a doctor like him.

But Ernest didn't want to go to college. He wanted to experience more of life. Sitting in a classroom for at least four more years was not the kind of experience he was looking for.

One of Ernest's uncles had a friend who worked for the *Kansas City Star* newspaper. That friend helped Ernest get a job as a reporter in the fall of 1917.

The *Kansas City Star* office

In October that year, Ernest moved to Kansas City, Missouri. He began reporting on news from the courthouse. However, it wasn't very exciting to write about judges and jury trials. He wanted to be where the action was! So he convinced his boss to assign him to crime reporting. That meant he would rush to the scene of a crime when the police were called.

It also meant covering the local hospital, where he wrote dramatic stories about accident victims.

Ernest liked working at the newspaper, but most important, he learned a particular way of writing at the *Star*. The newspaper had a style that it wanted all its reporters to follow. The rules were detailed in what is called a style guide.

Ernest learned to write that way in his crime stories. And he used the newspaper's style for the rest of his life.

Rules to Write By

More than twenty years after Ernest Hemingway worked at the *Kansas City Star*, he said that the newspaper taught him "the best rules I ever learned for the business of writing."

A few of the main rules were:

USE SHORT SENTENCES
That makes it easier for the reader.

USE SHORT FIRST PARAGRAPHS

They help the reader understand the main point of a story.

USE VIGOROUS ENGLISH

Choose words that are full of energy.

BE POSITIVE, NOT NEGATIVE

Focus on what something is, not what it isn't.

ELIMINATE EVERY SUPERFLUOUS WORD

Superfluous means something extra that is not necessary.

AVOID THE USE OF ADJECTIVES

The newspaper wanted just the facts.

CHAPTER 3
Love and War

In 1914, when World War I began in Europe, Ernest was still in high school. For a long time, the United States stayed out of the war. But in 1917, America entered the fight.

Like many young men his age, Ernest was eager to join the war effort. But when he went to sign up for the army, he was turned down. His eyesight was bad.

Still, Ernest wanted to do his part for his country. In 1918, he joined the American Red Cross, which helped bring supplies and medical services to soldiers. Ernest volunteered to drive ambulances in Italy for the Red Cross. It was dangerous work. Ernest would transport wounded soldiers with the battle going on all

around him. That didn't scare him. He wanted to "see if I can find out where the war is," he said. By driving an ambulance, he would be near the front lines and see the fighting firsthand. But Ernest's view of war was too simple. He thought of it as another adventure. Courage and bravery were all that mattered. Right away, Ernest found out how wrong he was.

World War I

World War I began in 1914 after a Serbian citizen murdered the archduke of Austria-Hungary. That angered Germany, which was an ally, or friend, of Austria-Hungary. Germany declared war on Russia, which was an ally of Serbia. Many other nations chose sides, and much of the world was soon at war.

The United States tried to stay out of World War I. But after German submarines (called U-boats) sank several American ships in 1917, the United States entered the war on the side of the Allied Powers: Great Britain, France, Italy, Russia, Japan, China, and more. They were fighting against the Central Powers, which included Germany, Austria-Hungary, and Turkey.

World War I—also called the Great War—was the deadliest war in history at the time. It lasted four years. More than sixteen million people were killed. The war finally ended in November 1918, when Germany was the last of the Central Powers to surrender.

Soldiers during World War I

On his first day in Italy, he heard a loud explosion from several miles away. A bomb destroyed a factory that made weapons. Many people who worked at the factory were killed. It was a terrible scene. Ernest helped recover many of the dead bodies.

About a month later, Ernest was delivering supplies to Italian soldiers on the front lines. A bomb exploded near Ernest and some soldiers. One man was killed. Another was badly injured. Ernest was hurt, too. His leg and knee were hit. Ernest said doctors later found more than two hundred pieces of shrapnel— small metal pieces of the bomb—in his leg.

Despite Ernest's injured leg, a friend reported that he carried the wounded soldier to a safe place. Ernest couldn't remember doing that. He had collapsed and lost consciousness. He was taken to a hospital in Milan, a large city in Italy.

Ernest was soon well enough to leave the hospital. However, that didn't mean he was strong enough to return to duty. He still needed a cane to get around on his injured leg. So the Red Cross sent him back home to the United States in January 1919.

Ernest returned to Oak Park. He had been one of the first Americans injured in Italy in the war. He also had been given a medal for bravery with the Red Cross, and the people of his hometown greeted him as a hero. Ernest loved the attention. He told a newspaper reporter that he had served in the Italian army, that the King of Italy personally gave him his medal, and that he had twelve surgeries for his war wounds. None of that was true, but those details made good stories. And even if the stories were exaggerated, Ernest had faced death with courage. Many characters in his future books would do the same.

Ernest was now a celebrity in his hometown, but he wanted something more. He needed a purpose in his life. He needed direction. And he wanted adventure. He didn't expect to find that in small-town Oak Park.

In early 1920, he moved to Toronto, Canada. He began writing articles for the *Toronto Star* newspaper. In October that year, he returned to the United States, to the city of Chicago. He was only about ten miles from Oak Park, but Chicago was a world of difference away.

Chicago, Illinois, 1920

It was then, and still is, the biggest city in Illinois, and one of the largest in the United States. Ernest wrote articles about farming for a magazine and lived with a friend from his Red Cross days.

At a party in Chicago, Ernest met Elizabeth Hadley Richardson. She lived in St. Louis, Missouri, but was visiting friends. Ernest was twenty-one by then. Hadley was twenty-nine. But they fell in love. Nine months later, they were married.

CHAPTER 4
To Paris

Sherwood Anderson

One of Ernest's friends in Chicago was Sherwood Anderson, a popular book author. Anderson convinced Ernest that if he really wanted to become a serious writer, he should move to Paris. Many American writers lived and worked there after the war. Anderson himself had recently come from Paris, where he was a friend of famous writers and poets such as F. Scott Fitzgerald, Gertrude Stein, James Joyce, Ezra Pound, and T. S. Eliot. Ernest and Hadley set sail for Europe on December 8, 1921.

They arrived in Paris twelve days later.

Anderson gave Ernest a letter of introduction to take with him. That's a polite way for a person to ask his or her friends to treat a stranger as a friend. With that letter, Ernest met many important writers and poets. He became good friends with F. Scott Fitzgerald, who would go on to write *The Great Gatsby*, and he taught poet Ezra Pound, a small and quiet man, how to box.

Ernest Hemingway and F. Scott Fitzgerald

The Lost Generation

Gertrude Stein

Writer Gertrude Stein called Ernest Hemingway and his American friends in Paris "the Lost Generation." Ernest helped make the phrase famous when he used it in his writing.

Stein meant that these young, creative people

were looking for direction and meaning in their lives. They weren't as interested in settling down to a quiet home and family life like previous generations often had been. They had lived through the horror of World War I and saw too many lives end early. So they traveled as much as they could, looking for new experiences and adventures.

Since Ernest's time, the phrase is used to refer to anyone who became an adult around the time of World War I, which lasted from 1914 to 1918.

During this time, Ernest wrote many articles for the Canadian newspaper the *Toronto Daily Star*. He took a train to Switzerland for a story about a major peace conference. He interviewed Italian leader Benito Mussolini in Milan. He reported from Western Asia on a war between Greece and Turkey.

Ernest interviews Benito Mussolini

In December 1922, Ernest was on an assignment for the *Toronto Daily Star* in Switzerland. He was earning a good salary writing and sending his articles back to Canada. But he wanted to work more on his short stories. So he asked Hadley, who was back in Paris, to send them to him. Hadley decided to surprise Ernest and visit him instead. She packed up all of his writing and stuffed it into a briefcase. She took the briefcase with her to the train station in Paris. But when Hadley reached her train compartment, the briefcase wasn't with the rest of her luggage. It had been lost—or stolen! The briefcase was never recovered. All of Ernest's stories were gone.

Hadley felt awful. She cried and cried. But Ernest really loved her. He felt worse about Hadley feeling bad than he did about losing his work.

Soon after, Ernest took a full-time job with the *Toronto Daily Star* and moved to Canada in early 1923. Before leaving Europe, he visited Spain, where he saw his first bullfight. It would be one of his passions for the rest of his life.

In Toronto, Ernest and Hadley had a son in October 1923. His birth name was John, but they called him either Jack or "Bumby," which was his nickname. Ernest, in fact, gave many people nicknames. He even gave himself one! He didn't like his first name, so sometime in the 1920s he began calling himself "Papa."

For a couple of months after Bumby was born, Ernest continued to write for the *Toronto Daily Star*. In addition, he still made time to finish his first book, *Three Stories and Ten Poems*.

Ernest, Hadley, and Bumby

But he felt he needed to concentrate full-time on his stories if he was to become a successful fiction writer. So in December, Ernest quit his job with the paper. He moved to Paris again with Hadley and Bumby.

At first, life back in Paris was difficult. Ernest

had no steady job, so the family had very little money. He spent much time admiring art in the famous museums in Paris. "When you've got a hungry gut and the museum is free, you go to the museum," he told a reporter.

Each day, Ernest would visit one of Paris's cafés and would work on his stories while sipping coffee or a drink. One time, a customer who was a former boxer brought in a pet lion. The owner asked the man not to bring in the lion anymore. The lion was quiet, but it scared the customers. Still, the man came back with his lion the very next day. And then again the next. Finally, Ernest took matters into his own hands. He threw the man out of the café. Then he came back for the lion, grabbed it by its mane, and led it outside. According to Ernest, "the lion gave me a look, but he went quietly."

At least, that's the way Ernest told the story.

Sometimes, Ernest was frustrated with his writing. He would look out at the city and tell himself not to worry. "You have always written before and you will write now," he thought. "All you have to do is write one true sentence. Write the truest sentence that you know."

Ernest figured that if one sentence came to him, more would follow. He was right. He completed several more books of short stories that were published in the United States over the next couple of years. But he believed he needed to write a novel in order to be taken seriously as a writer.

He needed only six weeks to finish his first  novel, *The Sun Also Rises*. One reason it was completed so quickly was that much of it was based on his own experiences. The book was about a group of young Americans living in Paris. They ate at the city's cafés, traveled to Spain, and talked about life—everything he did with his own friends.

The names were different, but many of

Ernest's friends recognized parts of themselves in *The Sun Also Rises*. Not all were happy about the book. But many critics praised it. "It is magnificent writing," said a reviewer in the *New York Times*. Words such as "amazing," "real," and "alive" were used to describe Ernest's writing.

The Sun Also Rises made Ernest a star. Unfortunately, things weren't going as well at home. Ernest wanted to be the best writer in the world. That meant work became the most important thing to him. And that meant Hadley and Bumby were not as important. He began spending less time with them. He met another woman, named Pauline Pfeiffer, and they fell in love.

Pauline Pfeiffer

Ernest and Hadley divorced in 1927.

Still, Ernest never stopped caring for Hadley. He gave the money he earned from writing *The Sun Also Rises* to her and Bumby.

CHAPTER 5
World Traveler

Ernest and Pauline were married in the spring of 1927. Over the next several years, they traveled all over the world. They went on a honeymoon to the Mediterranean. They went to Germany to watch bicycle races, to Spain to watch bullfights, and to New York to watch boxing and football. They went skiing in Switzerland and sightseeing in Cuba. In 1928, they moved to Key West, Florida.

Key West is an island surrounded by the Atlantic Ocean. It is known for outdoor activities such as hiking, fishing, and snorkeling. It is very different from a large, sophisticated city like Paris. In Key West, Ernest became a fisherman, especially of large fish such as tuna, marlin, and swordfish, entering contests and winning awards. He practiced his boxing. Sometimes, he would offer money to anyone in Key West who could last three rounds with him in the ring. No one could do it.

Any hobbies he enjoyed came after Ernest was done writing for the day. Every morning, he would get up very early, at five or six o'clock. He stood before a bookshelf in his room. Atop the bookshelf was a typewriter and whatever story or novel he was working on. Ernest liked to work standing up.

Ernest began by reading over everything he had already written to that point in each story. By the time he finished a manuscript, he had read it over many, many times, making changes along the way.

Ernest worked hard for several hours. He did not want any disturbances while he wrote. By noon, he was done writing for the day. When he was finished, he noted on the wall above the bookshelf how many words he had written.

In this way, Ernest began writing *A Farewell to Arms* while in Key West. It was another book that had many elements of Ernest's own life in it.

A Farewell to Arms was about an American lieutenant who drove an ambulance in Italy during World War I, was injured, and fell in love with his nurse. The "arms" in the title can be taken to mean either the weapons of war or the arms of a loved one.

Before Ernest finished writing *A Farewell to Arms*, he learned that his father had died. Ernest loved his father. He had lovely memories of good times with him. But he also had bad memories of his father disciplining

him. Ernest's relationship with his own sons was similarly good and bad. After Jack, Patrick was born to him and Pauline in 1928. A third son, Gregory, was born three years later. Ernest admitted he was not a great father—even though his nickname was "Papa"! It was complicated. His children admired him and enjoyed being around him. When they were together, Ernest taught them to hunt and fish, just like his father had taught him. He was proud of them and bragged about them to his friends.

But since Ernest spent most of his time traveling and writing, he was not around them very often.

After his father's funeral, Ernest returned to Key West to finish *A Farewell to Arms*. It was first published one chapter at a time in *Scribner's* magazine, then in book form. "Here is genius," wrote one book reviewer in the *Chicago Tribune*. "At the age of thirty-one, he is already a legendary figure," wrote a columnist in the *Boston Globe*. The publisher of *A Farewell to Arms* printed thirty-one thousand copies in September 1929. Those copies sold out in just a few weeks. The same month, the book was reprinted twice. Those copies sold out, too. Another printing followed in October, then three more in November.

Every time Ernest finished writing a book, he took time to unwind. He and Pauline went on fishing trips to Cuba, spent time on a ranch in Montana, and visited Spain to watch the bullfights and the running of the bulls.

In 1932, Ernest wrote a book about bullfighting

called *Death in the Afternoon*. It was a true account of the tradition of bullfighting and the passion some cultures have for it.

Ernest and Pauline at the running of the bulls

The title of the book refers to both the death of the bull and the danger of death a bullfighter, called a *matador*, faces. In a bullfight, the matador attempts to kill the animal in a circular arena called the bullring. The most skilled matadors do this by daring to get as close to the bull as possible, putting themselves in danger.

Death in the Afternoon went into great detail about matadors and their techniques. In the book, Ernest also wrote his thoughts about life, death, and bravery.

Today, many people believe that bullfighting is simply cruelty to animals. For that reason, it is now illegal in many parts of the world. However, in some places in Spain, Mexico, and other parts of Latin America, bullfighting is considered an art form. Ernest thought it was, too. He saw it as a test of courage for the matador. He made many trips to Spain and became friends with several matadors, some who were as famous in Spain at that time as movie stars are today.

The running of the bulls is now a big tourist attraction in Pamplona, Spain, in part because of Ernest. His books *The Sun Also Rises* and *Death in the Afternoon* helped bring the festival worldwide attention. The tradition started several hundreds of years ago in Spain, when bulls had to be led from the farms to the village market. It wasn't long before young men started competing to see who was brave and fast enough

to run ahead of the bulls without getting hurt. That appealed to Ernest, who often wrote about bravery in his characters.

When Ernest went to Spain with a group of his friends, he was always the ringleader, the man in charge. He would handle all the arrangements. He would decide where to stay, what to eat, and what to do. Most of the time, that was okay with everyone. But sometimes it was not. Some of his friends thought that the more famous Ernest became, the more overconfident he became. Friends who disagreed with him often found they weren't invited on any more trips. His arrogance seemed to lead to accidents wherever he traveled, including an eye infection in Italy and a serious car accident in Montana. For Ernest, these were simply the price one paid for always being on the go. "A life of action," he once said, "is much easier to me than writing."

CHAPTER 6
New Adventures

Ernest had now written three best-selling books. He was well known in Europe and the United States. Ernest's writing style was very different than other authors' at this time. He used simple words and phrases. People thought he didn't know "the ten-dollar words," he said, meaning big or fancy words. He also used fewer words to get his point across. "My aim," he said, "is to put down on paper what I see and what I feel in the best and simplest way."

Ernest's ninth book, 1933's *Winner Take Nothing*, was a collection of short stories. One of those stories was "A Clean, Well-Lighted Place." It is about an old man who is lonely and tries to kill himself but then finds comfort passing time in a café—a clean, well-lighted place. James Joyce, a famous Irish novelist, called it "one of the best short stories ever written." Ernest once said it may have been his favorite ever.

James Joyce reviews *Winner Take Nothing*

Still, writing wasn't enough for him. By then, Ernest also wanted a new adventure. In 1933, he and Pauline traveled to Kenya and Tanzania for a two-month safari.

Ernest had never been to Africa before, and he was amazed at what he saw. "Nothing that I have ever read has given any idea of the beauty of the country," he wrote at the time. However, Ernest wasn't there just to admire the scenery. He wanted to head into the countryside and hunt for big game: lions, hyenas, rhinos, leopards, and more. Ernest viewed it as the ultimate challenge of man versus beast.

Like bullfighting, big-game hunting has come to be seen in many parts of the world as cruel to animals. There are many laws now that limit this sort of hunting. But at the time, it was widely accepted and thought of as a sport for only the bravest hunters.

During the hunt, Ernest suffered from dysentery, a serious disease that causes diarrhea and severe stomach pains. Only a couple of weeks

into the safari, a plane was called to take him to Nairobi, the capital city of Kenya, for medical help. Along the way, the plane passed over Kilimanjaro, the highest mountain in Africa.

After a few days, Ernest felt better and returned to the safari. As usual, his experiences provided plenty of inspiration for his writing, including the most famous short story of his career, "The Snows of Kilimanjaro." It is about a dying writer who looks back at his life after being injured on an African safari.

Ernest was able to use his experiences in his work because he had an amazing memory. It was so good that he never kept notes or relied on a journal. "I just push the recall button and there it is," he said. "If it isn't there, it wasn't worth keeping."

After returning from Africa, Ernest bought a fishing boat he called *Pilar*. He sailed from Key West, Florida, to Cuba and back again on *Pilar*.

In 1935, he went deep-sea fishing to Bimini, the Bahamas. But along the way, Ernest accidentally shot himself in both legs while trying to get a shark he had hooked onto the boat!

All these accidents might have made another man slow down a bit. But Ernest had no interest in shying away from danger. In 1937, he agreed to report on the Spanish Civil War for the newspapers. The Spanish Civil War was fought between the Loyalists, who supported an elected government, and the Nationalists, who supported a dictatorship led by General Francisco Franco. In February 1937, Ernest set sail for Spain. He wrote his first reports from Madrid in March.

Ernest's war reporting sided clearly with the Loyalists. He even wrote the script for a war film called *The Spanish Earth*. The film blamed the Nationalists for the country's problems. That helped make Ernest a favorite among the Loyalists.

He was no longer such a favorite with his wife, Pauline, however. He often traveled without her. By the time the Spanish Civil War was over in

1939, he was living with Martha Gellhorn, a newspaper reporter. In 1940, Ernest officially divorced Pauline and married Martha.

Ernest with Martha Gellhorn

Ernest and Martha lived in a house near Havana, the capital city of Cuba. Ernest loved living in Cuba. His home there, called the Finca Vigía (which means "lookout farm" in Spanish),

Finca Vigía

was built on a hill. From the back of the house, Ernest had a beautiful view of the city of Havana, fifteen miles away.

At the Finca Vigía, Ernest wrote *For Whom the Bell Tolls*, a novel about an American teacher who travels to Spain to fight on the side of the Loyalists in the Spanish Civil War. The book was one

of the top five best-selling books in the United States in both 1940 and 1941. It is considered a classic and is still widely read today.

Ernest, now in his early forties, still liked to write in the morning,

finishing by noon. Then it was time for lunch, followed by a nap and a daily swim in the pool. He was close enough to walk to the docks to take *Pilar* out on the water. A constant stream of friends came by for dinner, before a short ride into Havana for drinking, singing, and storytelling in the city.

And everywhere, there were cats. About twenty-five cats lived at the Finca Vigía, and Ernest knew the names of all of them. Later, he also had a springer spaniel named Black Dog, who faithfully kept him company during his writing hours. With his pets, Ernest showed a softer side of himself than the image he had as a daring and adventurous man of action.

CHAPTER 7
War Correspondent

While Ernest was enjoying life in Havana, the world was becoming more unsettled. World War II began in Europe in 1939. At the time, the United States and Cuba were not officially involved.

That all changed after December 7, 1941, when Japanese planes bombed Pearl Harbor in Hawaii. The very next day, the United States officially joined the war. One day after that, Cuba also joined. The United States and Cuba were on the side of the Allies, which included Great Britain, Russia, and China. They were fighting the Axis powers, which included Germany, Italy, and Japan.

With Japan's attack on Pearl Harbor, the war in Europe finally reached North America.

German U-boats had been patrolling the Atlantic Ocean since the war began. A U-boat, which is short for the German word for "undersea boat," was a military submarine. It could travel undetected underwater and shoot a deadly torpedo to sink an enemy ship. Now that the United States officially was in the war, the German U-boat patrols in the Atlantic spread.

U-boat

Ernest was too old to join the service, but he sensed a new adventure. He asked the US government to allow him to carry machine guns and hand grenades on the *Pilar* to hunt German U-boats. Ernest went to great lengths to hide the guns and grenades. He wanted the *Pilar* to look like any other fishing boat. And, according to Ernest, he provided the US government with "good information" about where U-boats were lurking.

Martha was assigned by *Collier's* magazine to report on the war from China. She also had war assignments in Hong Kong, Finland, and more. Ernest was jealous. So in 1944, he traveled to London, also writing for *Collier's*.

Once in Europe, Ernest didn't just sit in a hotel room writing magazine articles. He went with British pilots on bombing missions for the Royal Air Force. He accompanied a US Army infantry division in France. He was there when US tanks rolled into Germany late in the war. But he seemed to be less interested in reporting than in being at the center of the action.

Royal Air Force planes from World War II

And the truth was, Martha was a better war reporter than Ernest. While Ernest reported on the famous D-Day landings in Normandy from a boat filled with other newspapermen, Martha sneaked onto a hospital ship and actually went ashore in France. In those days, women were not

allowed in combat. She was the only woman to land on the beach at Normandy on June 6, 1944, as more than three million troops from twelve Allied nations crossed the English Channel from Great Britain to France, which had been held by Germany since June 1940.

Martha Ellis Gellhorn (1908–1998)

Martha Gellhorn was one of the best—if not the best—war reporters of her time.

Martha was born in St. Louis, Missouri, and attended Bryn Mawr College in Pennsylvania. She wrote for *The New Republic* magazine and then began writing about crime for a newspaper in Albany, New York.

In 1937, Martha traveled to Spain to cover the Spanish Civil War for *Collier's* magazine. She was one of the first female war reporters for a US publication. She would go on to cover many wars around the world over the next several decades, including World War II, the Korean War, and the Vietnam War.

Martha was known mostly for exploring stories of ordinary people in her war reporting. But she also wrote novels and many short stories.

Ernest never got over his competition with Martha. He was hurt that her career was more important to her than their relationship—even though his own travels and career had ruined his past relationships.

Ernest and Martha divorced in 1945, but it wasn't long before he married again. In 1946, Mary Welsh became his fourth wife. She was a reporter, too. They had met in London during the war.

Ernest and Mary were very famous. They traveled all over the world. In Italy, Ernest took his new wife to the place where he had been wounded in World War I. They skied in France and Switzerland. They hunted in Idaho. Their friends were famous, too, and included actresses, artists, and European royalty.

Among his friends, Ernest was easy to recognize, with his distinctive white beard. The nickname "Papa" seemed to fit him well.

Ernest with Mary Welsh

Once, while at the bullfights in Spain with Mary, the crowd recognized him and gave him a standing ovation. The fans remembered how he had sided with the rebels against the Nationalists in the Spanish Civil War and how he wrote passionately about bullfighting.

CHAPTER 8
Triumph and Tragedy

At one point during World War II, a reader poll in *The Saturday Review of Literature* named Ernest the best novelist in the United States. But Ernest wasn't writing much at that time. After *For Whom the Bell Tolls* was published in 1940, it was ten years before Ernest produced another novel. And it wasn't his best effort.

In 1950, *Across the River and into the Trees* was Ernest's fifteenth book. It is about a US Army officer in Italy who looks back at his life. Although it was popular with the public, reviewers did not like it. "A bitter disappointment," said one typical review.

It was the first time Ernest's work was so poorly reviewed, and he was stung by the criticism.

He was struggling in his personal life as well. Ernest injured his head in a boating accident in Cuba in 1950. He also injured his leg and his foot in a car accident that same year. In 1951, Ernest's

Charles Scribner

mother, Grace, died. So did Pauline, his second wife. Charles Scribner, his longtime publisher and one of his best friends, passed away in 1952.

"The time to prove what you are made of is not when you are at the top of your form," he told a friend, "but when you've been knocked [down] and you have to get up off the canvas. So the time has come for a counterattack."

Ernest's counterattack was his next book, *The*

Old Man and the Sea. The short novel is about a Cuban fisherman who had gone eighty-four days without catching a fish before battling a huge Atlantic blue marlin for three days and nights. It is a simply told story that Ernest had been thinking about for years. "The best I can write ever for all of my life," Ernest said about the book. It became his most widely read work.

The Old Man and the Sea originally was printed in *Life* magazine in 1952. The magazine sold more than five million copies in the first two days it was on newsstands.

"He had reclaimed his position," said A. E. Hotchner, a writer friend of Ernest's. "It was like a champ who had lost his title and he comes back in a rematch and proves that he is the champ."

The Old Man and the Sea won the Pulitzer Prize for fiction in 1953. The next year, Ernest was awarded the Nobel Prize in Literature. Each honor came with a cash award, too. Ernest was rich. He was famous. He was at the height of his career.

Ernest didn't write much after *The Old Man and the Sea*. Still, the legend of "Papa" continued to grow.

Ernest receiving his Nobel Prize

In the late 1950s, Ernest and Mary moved to Ketchum, Idaho. Ernest had several friends there, and he could once again hunt and fish. Ernest took with him the contents of two pieces of his luggage the Ritz Hotel in Paris found in 1956.

He had accidentally left the luggage behind almost thirty years earlier. Some of his old clothes were packed inside. But there also were notes, newspaper clippings, and stories he had worked on in the 1920s.

Ernest decided to use them to write a book about his days in Paris as a young man. "Writing is the only thing that makes me feel that I'm not wasting my time sticking around," he said.

But the writing process was slow because Ernest was not well. He had been injured many  times. He was drinking too much alcohol. Ernest's doctor told him to quit drinking, but he didn't. He knew his days of adventure were over.

However, Ernest was used to being a strong and daring man. He didn't want to slow down. "If I can't exist on my own terms, then existence is impossible," he said late in his life. By the summer of 1961, Ernest felt like he could no longer write. His health prevented him from having the wild and sometimes dangerous experiences he wanted, and his memory was fading. He could no longer recall his past adventures. On the morning of July 2, 1961, Ernest died by suicide in Ketchum.

He left behind his wife, Mary; his three children; and several grandchildren. He also left behind friends all over the world, having lived in places as varied as Paris, Havana, Key West, and Ketchum. And, of course, he left behind his readers, who numbered in the millions.

Ernest was gone, but his writing has lived on. Three years after his death, Mary helped finish putting together *A Moveable Feast*, the book about Ernest's years in Paris. Several other books and stories found among Ernest's belongings were published in the years after his death.

Mary with a copy of *A Moveable Feast*

Today, there are Hemingway writing contests around the world and walking tours in Paris, Madrid, and other cities that Ernest wrote about.

Contestants at the Hemingway look-alike contest celebrate

His homes in Oak Park, Florida, and Cuba have been turned into museums. The town of Key West even holds an annual Hemingway look-alike contest. His writing is still taught in schools across the United States, and his books are still read around the world.

"You invent fiction," he once said, "but what you invent it out of is what counts. True fiction must come from everything you've ever known, ever seen, ever felt, ever learned."

Ernest knew, saw, felt, and learned many things in his life. More than most people, he lived life as a grand adventure.

If you, or someone you know, is struggling with mental health or thinking about suicide, please call one of the twenty-four-hour crisis hotline numbers below right away.

1-800-662-HELP (4357)
Substance Abuse and Mental Health Services Administration

1-800-273-TALK (8255)
National Suicide Prevention Lifeline

Timeline of Ernest Hemingway's Life

1899 — Ernest Hemingway is born on July 21 in Oak Park, Illinois

1917 — Moves to Kansas City

1918 — Becomes an ambulance driver in Italy in World War I

1921 — Marries his first wife, Elizabeth Hadley Richardson

— Moves to Paris to write

1926 — His first novel, *The Sun Also Rises*, is published

1927 — Divorces Hadley and marries Pauline Pfeiffer

1928 — Moves to Key West

1929 — *A Farewell to Arms* is printed in *Scribner's* magazine

1937 — Covers the Spanish Civil War for an American newspaper group

1939 — Moves to Cuba

1940 — Divorces Pauline and marries Martha Gellhorn

— *For Whom the Bell Tolls* is published

1945 — Divorces Martha

1946 — Marries Mary Welsh

1952 — *The Old Man and the Sea* is published

1953 — Wins the Pulitzer Prize in fiction for *The Old Man and the Sea*

1954 — Awarded the Nobel Prize in Literature

1961 — Dies on July 2 in Ketchum, Idaho

Timeline of the World

1903 — Orville and Wilbur Wright make the first powered flight at Kitty Hawk, North Carolina

1912 — The ocean liner RMS *Titanic* sinks on its first voyage

1914 — World War I begins

1918 — A major flu pandemic begins, eventually killing as many as fifty million people around the world

1920 — The Nineteenth Amendment gives US women the right to vote

1929 — The stock market crashes in the United States, and the Great Depression begins

1932 — Franklin Delano Roosevelt is elected president of the United States for the first of a record four terms

1945 — The US drops atomic bombs on the Japanese cities Hiroshima and Nagasaki in August, leading to the end of World War II

1947 — Jackie Robinson becomes the first Black player in the modern era of Major League Baseball

1955 — Rosa Parks, a Black woman, is arrested in Birmingham, Alabama, for refusing to give up her seat on a bus to a white passenger, fueling the modern civil rights movement

Bibliography

*Books for young readers

Hemingway, Ernest. ***A Moveable Feast (The Restored Edition)***.
New York, NY: Scribner, 2010.

Hotchner, A. E. ***Papa Hemingway: A Personal Memoir***.
Cambridge, MA: Da Capo Press, 2005.

*Lyttle, Richard B. ***Ernest Hemingway: The Life and the Legend***.
New York, NY: Atheneum, 1992.

Mellow, James R. ***Hemingway: A Life Without Consequences***.
Boston, MA: Houghton Mifflin, 1992.

Oliver, Charles M. ***Ernest Hemingway A to Z***. New York, NY:
Checkmark Books, 1999.

*Pratt, Paula Bryant. ***The Importance of Ernest Hemingway***.
San Diego, CA: Lucent Books, 1999.

*Reef, Catherine. ***Ernest Hemingway: A Writer's Life***. Boston, MA:
Clarion Books, 2009.

Sandison, David. ***Ernest Hemingway: An Illustrated Biography***.
London: Hamlyn, 1998.

Vejdovsky, Boris, with Mariel Hemingway. ***Hemingway: A Life in
Pictures***. Richmond Hill, ON: Firefly Books, 2011.